My Name is Dick

DICK SHERROD

Copyright © 2020 by Dick Sherrod

All rights reserved

No part of this book may be reproduced or transmitted in any form or by any means without written permission of the author.

Published with Assistance from
Writer Book Publishing Services
www.writerbookpublishing.com

Printed and bound in the
United States of America

ISBN: 978-1-734689-1-12

My Name Is Dick
By Dick Sherrod

My Name Is Dick

Dedication

For all the Bills that aren't Williams,

Kathys and Katys that aren't Katherines,

John & Jacks that aren't Roberts,

Drews that aren't Andrews,

Nickis that aren't Nicoles

Rickys that aren't Richards

Billys that aren't Williams

Tommys that aren't Thomas,

and especially, to

Dicks that aren't Richards.

Acknowledgments

Thanks to all those who encouraged me over the years to document my "Dick" stories – especially all of my former work associates, friends, neighbors, and life partner, Norman. They will each remember several of the tales documented here – and some were even present for one or more of these stories! A special shout out to Christine who introduced me to my writing and publishing mentor, Michelle Owens, without whom this book may have never happened. Love you Mo!!

Contents

Dedication iii

Acknowledgments i

Contents ii

Introduction 1

Proving I'm a Real Dick 5

The Long and Colorful History of Dick (or Even If You Think You Do, You Don't Know Dick) 9

If Your Name is Dick, Don't Be One 29

See Dick Work 39

Everyday Dick 54

See Dick Travel 68

You Can't Have a Dick and a Smile, But You Might Get a Lyft 87

Concluding Thoughts 92

About The Author 94

Introduction

For Dicks like me, each new day brings another story. As the baby boomers grow older and the workforce is now full of millennials, gen X, Y, and now Z humans, new writing material for this book seems to grow daily. In the past when dealing with my own generation and those before, there was never really a shock and awe factor surrounding my name. Even though most Dicks, Dickys, Dickies, and Dickeys were really Richards who had been nicknamed, simply hearing, writing or speaking one of Dick's variations was fairly common and didn't raise many eyebrows. With the passage of time and the movement of my name into commonplace slang for penis, imbeciles, and idiots, that changed. It was actually the use of my name for the most important of male organs that has most caused my name to be embarrassing for many to say.

Each time I am required to fill out a document, make a

My Name Is Dick

reservation, sign in, apply for credit, title a home, property or car, sign up for insurance, and the list goes on and on, Dick is usually a subject of question. I usually get some type of call, instant message popup, bad language warning, or something occurring regarding the use of my name, Dick. I have had to make countless corrections, affirmations and/or requests over the years for my name. It is now such a daily routine of my life that often I barely even register it.

Even though my name is Dick, my nickname was Dickey all the way through high school. Everyone only knew me by Dickey. It wasn't until college that I began to drop my nickname and go by Dick. It was at that time the daily routine and trials of not being a Richard started, albeit it wasn't because of my name being associated with a penis. It was more for the array of celebrities and politicians that were all Richards that called themselves Dick.

Over time, I've come to realize that my name alone has been enough to carve out a unique life path for me. My every day is very different from most people's -- simply because I'm a Dick.

There is not a day that passes when I can avoid facing some of the big questions and decisions of life, ones surrounding shame, acceptance, prudes, and political correctness. About picking my battles. About how to put others at ease, or how to turn weaknesses into strengths. About finding the ability to handle the multitude of awkwardnesses imposed regularly upon me.

My Name Is Dick

Long ago, I discovered that laughing at my vulnerabilities was the first step to embracing them, and as I began to embrace my vulnerabilities, I embraced true happiness. Once I began to wear my name loud and proud, my career, personal happiness and well-being blossomed. I began to tell everyone that I was going to document my journey in the future. My name became a part of what made me who I am today. And today, I couldn't be happier than to be a Real Dick. Loud and proud.

Writing down my stories is the culmination of a lifelong journey of learning not only to accept myself, but to celebrate it all.

I'm finally one happy Dick.

There is another reason why I want to talk about Dick. Someday, all the Dicks will be gone. Even today, we are exceedingly rare. Most people under 30 simply don't believe Dick is a real name -- or that my parents weren't whack jobs bent on ruining my life from birth. They are baffled that it was ever popular. I want to explore and document the story of my name, how its popularity rose and fell, and what it meant to live with a name that didn't change while its meaning did. It's been quite a journey.

And besides, since I like to put people at ease and make them laugh, I've long counted on my name to give me a new dinner party story. It's my hope that you will find the Dick stories entertaining, too -- and maybe even a little insightful and helpful. I hope you enjoy reading about them as much as I enjoyed telling

My Name Is Dick

them.

We all have our challenges. Mine just happens to be that I'm a Real Dick.

Welcome, friends, to the party!

Only one thing -- we won't be serving any Coca-cola. So pour any other beverage of your choice, and enjoy. I will explain my anti-Coke stance before we're through.

Dick Sherrod

Proving I'm a Real Dick

I am going to start here, because at some point we're going to have to get this out of the way. I always do when I meet people.

Sooner or later, I have to prove I'm a Real Dick. Not Richard. Dick.

I will be at a neighborhood party where I know most of the guests -- but inevitably, there will be a new one to show up, and the unavoidable introductions begin. If I'm lucky, I will get in a half-glass of wine before the subject of my name comes up.

"...and his name really is Dick," one of my friends will say to the new neighbor, introducing me. I've learned not to wince, and while the reaction of the new acquaintance can vary, there is almost always one commonality. Disbelief.

This is when I quietly reach into my wallet, pull out my

My Name Is Dick

license, and hand it to them. Here it is, now, for you. Only I don't know you well enough to give you my other personal data, so I've blurred it out. But yes, I am a man, I live in Florida, and to the point -- my name is Dick.

"Wow, what's that like?" Will be the comment most folks give.

For some people, however, and definitely to the TSA (that story later) and even some websites, my license is not enough proof. "Couldn't Dick be a nickname and still on your license?" I'm asked.

"I don't know," I will reply, "It's not my nickname."

No, I don't keep my birth certificate in my wallet, but there have been times when I wish I did. I can include it for you.

My Name Is Dick

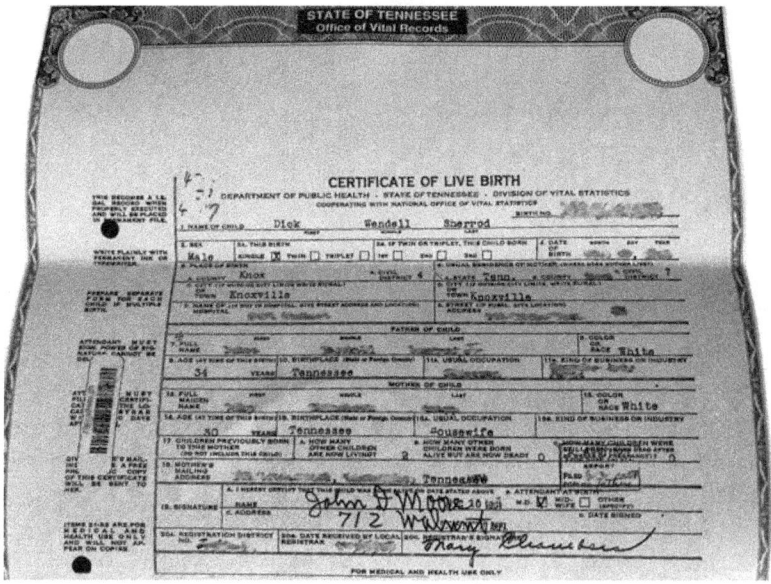

So now, while you might not have my birth date or address, you have the notarized proof that I am most definitely a Real Dick.

Besides, who would make this up? Not the draft board, that's for sure.

My Name Is Dick

Not that I am a Dick about this. Oh wait. I am. I can't help it.

The Long and Colorful History of Dick (or Even If You Think You Do, You Don't Know Dick)

"Dick. 1. A dictionary."

I put my head on my desk and laughed at the definition. Maybe I was a little punchy. By the time I got to reviewing the definition of dick to mean dictionary from the 1905 Dictionary of Slang and Colloquial English by John S. Farmer and W.E. Henley, I was weeks into studying about the history of the word and name dick. If it was your much-maligned name, you might be a little obsessed too.

My Name Is Dick

Yes, I thought, my head still resting on my desk. Dick as dictionary is about right. Who knew the history of a simple group of four letters could be so lengthy and varied?

Okay -- so the linguists (who make a career out of understanding words) and the onomasticians (who study proper names) knew. Interviews with them gave me my first indication that tracing the etymology of dick was not going to be the straightforward task I had first imagined.

I had thought that anyone named Dick knew it was a name, and everyone else knew it meant penis. All I had to find out how it went from one to another, and I would understand everything there was to know about the word, right?

Wrong.

As Dr. Michael Adams, professor of English at Indiana University Bloomington and author of *Slang: The People's Poetry* said in his interview, "It's very hard to figure out exactly where any word comes from, and slang etymology is even harder. It can be painstaking."

As I dug into research, I began to understand what Dr. Adams meant. Complicating the overlapping histories of Dick the name and dick the word is its multitude of past slang meanings as an abbreviated or rhyming version of numerous other words, all of which pre-date its use as a word for penis, and stand apart from its use as a name.

My Name Is Dick

I must say, this has restored a bit of pride for my much-maligned name.

Before my research, I had only known one alternate meaning of dick, and it was British. Across the pond, "dick" also means pudding -- and has for centuries. There's no evidence that the uses of dick as pudding and dick as penis are at all related. (Though, as we'll see, the dessert is now a source of some British embarrassment.) It is far more likely that dick as a pudding is simply a shortened version of the old English spelling for the word pudding -- which was, no surprise, puddick.

Then I looked in the *Oxford English Dictionary*, where I learned that dick has also acted as an abbreviated version of "declaration," as in "the man issued his dying dick." Once again, this historical use of the word dick was unrelated to its other many uses, but if today, however, someone told me they had a "dying dick," I wouldn't be thinking about a will. I'd be thinking about the awkward pharmaceutical ads targeting older men, the ones which always come on during sports games. Call your doctor if this seems right for you.

In the 1860's, you could tell people that you got your horse to move by using your dick, and no one would think you were the least bit creepy. Dick was then a term for a riding whip or crop. Don't even go there, now, please and for the love of all that is holy.

In late 18th century America, dick referred to Irish Catholics.

My Name Is Dick

I have not been able to find out why -- but it's possible that this meaning for dick has something to do with how dick and Catholic rhyme.

And then there's the historically-popular slang phrases which make me grin despite myself. Are you "up to dick?" In the 1870s, this would mean you excel, hitting the mark at whatever you are attempting. Of course, no one wants to be "dicked in the nob" (1820s for crazy). Are you going to pledge an oath in the 1860s? Then you're about to "take one's dick." Are you a WWI soldier who thinks you don't get paid enough? Then you're getting "money for dick."

Green's Dictionary of Slang gives at least 10 additional meanings for the word dick, including victim, weakling, and sexual partner.

I am not responsible for how you choose to use all this information.

I will say that I'm amazed at how dick is one amazing shape-shifter of a word. One might even go so far as to say that the word dick qualifies as dick, which also once meant "fine language."

From meaning fine language to becoming an obscenity, Dick also offers a clear lesson in how far something can fall.

Less clear is how the fall happened -- how dick came to mean penis. One possibility originates in dick's use as a stand-in for

My Name Is Dick

the word everyman. Another possibility is based upon dick's ability to rhyme with yet another word, one already established as an obscenity.

Shakespeare had established "prick" to mean penis long before dick was used to mean penis, and so, according to Dr. Frank Nuessel, professor of linguistics at the University of Louisville and author of *The Study of Names: A Guide to the Principles and Topics*, with the Brits' rhyming tendencies, taking "prick to dick would not be uncharacteristic."

Dr. Cleveland Evans, a professor at Nebraska's Bellevue University who specializes in onomastics and is past president of the American Name Society, agrees. Dr. Evans says, "I think the reason Dick got picked on was because it rhymed with prick, which predates it."

Dr. Adams, however, points out that "as Henry Mayhew found in the 1850's, rhyming slang was not a basic British tendency, but it was more common in the lives of the British poor."

If this is true, when dick was first published in 1836 as a word meaning penis, it probably came straight from the streets of London. This is further evidenced by the type of publication the word was found in -- a bawdy songbook meant to be kept out of polite society.

A Dictionary of Slang and Unconventional English by Eric Partridge says dick meant, among other uses, "the membrum virile"

My Name Is Dick

(a.k.a. penis) to members of the military starting around 1860.

Yet John Camden Hotten's Slang Dictionary, published nine years later in 1869, cites the riding whip, dictionary and Richard nickname meanings of dick, without any mention of the penis definition. It is possible that the penis use of dick was considered too crude for this 1869 publication, but the same edition of his dictionary, while not being explicit, does call one use of the word cock "vulgar." Nothing about dick is noted by Hotten even to be vulgar, so my deduction is this: that while dick could mean penis in the 1860's, that this usage was likely very limited, and limited to the British poor and the military.

Yet while the downfall of my name quietly began, my name and its predecessor Richard continued reigning supreme, as they had for centuries. To wit: according to Green, the earliest slang use of dick dates back to 1592, when it was first used to mean a generic term for "man" or "mankind." This use is attributable to the long-lived popularity of the name Richard, a name which first rose to prominence in England 1,000 years ago -- with Dick as one of its shortened versions. The nickname is so common that the phrase "Tom Dick and Harry" (dating to the 1700's) is another euphemism for men in general.

It's pretty straightforward to see how dick became an abbreviated form of a word like "dictionary" or "declaration," but how did Dick become an abbreviated form of the name Richard?

My Name Is Dick

Remember, according to Dr. Nuessel, the "British were famous for rhyming slang" -- so for Richard to evolve into Rick and then Dick makes sense. (This is also how William became Will and then Bill, and Robert became Rob and then Bob.)

However, to more fully understand the reign of any name -- at least in the United States -- the data the Social Security Administration (SSA) provides is invaluable, offering the popularity ranking of all names given to babies born each year since 1900. For some names, these numbers make it super easy to trace the reasons for a name's gain or loss in popularity. Take the name Ayra, for example. Never in the top 1000 names for girls before 2010, its rise in popularity correlates directly with that of *Game of Thrones* and the show-favorite character of the same name. Ayra broke into the list at #942 in 2010 (a few years after the first book came out and a year before the show first aired) and steadily continued to rise with the popularity of the series, becoming the 119th most popular name in 2018.

For the name Dick, however, direct lines to a single person (living or fictional) aren't as easy to draw. According to the SSA, Dick was at its peak popularity from 1927 to 1945 -- when it ranked continually in the top 100's of new baby names. While not as obvious as the *Game of Thrones* phenomenon, the biggest pop-culture correlation to Dick's popularity was the advent of the cartoon detective Dick Tracy, which debuted in 1931.

My Name Is Dick

Before Dick Tracy, dick had long been a word used to refer to detectives and investigators. Dick has also been slang for a clever fellow, and curiously, dick has been used as a verb to mean to look or watch something, often in a spying manner. (So I guess you could say Dick Tracy was a dick who did a lot of dicking.) Regardless, Tracy's exploits quickly rose to enduring cartoon fame. And the name seemed to ride high with him.

In 1940, during Dick's highest use as a name in the United States, a W.C. Fields comedy called *The Bank Dick* was released in theaters. It was about a bank guard -- hence the word dick in the title.

Something happened to this movie title, however, something which holds a clue to the growing use of dick as penis, and points once more to the Brits as the culprits. When dick was first used as a term meaning penis in 1800's England, it wasn't common, but I believe it had become so by 1940 -- for while *The Bank Dick* was running in the US, it was also released in Britain...under the name *The Bank Detective*. I couldn't find a definitive explanation for the title change, but one highly-plausible explanation was that enough Brits had caught on to the "inappropriate" usage of dick that it was considered too unseemly for a movie title.

Meanwhile, those of us in the United States were still blissfully unaware, happily using the name with our movies,

My Name Is Dick

cartoon characters, and kids.

This does indeed feel like detective -- or should I say dick -- work.

There are, thankfully, at least a few definitive moments which can be pointed to for clues for the fall of my name. The first is two world wars.

During World War I, British soldiers were already using dick to mean penis. They had informally renamed their D.S.O. (Distinguished Service Order) award to mean Dick Shot Off. By World War II, it appears the Americans had adopted this use of DSO. What's undisputed is that during both of these wars, the Americans picked up on and invented many slang terms. It would not be surprising if dick then, as penis, would be one of them.

Granted, the post-war baby boom ushered in a whole new era in baby names, but it is interesting how Dick fell out of the SSA's list of top 100 most popular names in the United States for the first time in 1946 -- just one year after World War II ended and the Americans returned home. Richard, however, was to remain strong for many years to come.

Dick's slide out of popularity as a name made it particularly vulnerable to becoming a target for slang use. "When you just hear John, you only think of the name, not its slang meaning, because John is still a common name," says Dr. Evans. "Dick went out of style in the 50's and early 60's. People started using Rick and Ricky.

My Name Is Dick

I believe it had something to do with *I Love Lucy.*"

The SSA name database backs this idea up. The height of Ricky as a given name was between 1958 and 1960, when it was in the top 30 most popular names -- and *I Love Lucy* was the number one show on television. During this period, Dick dropped from 504 to 574 in popularity, continuing its downward trend.

Also, it's likely that by the late 1950's, many more people in the US "knew the 'other' meaning of dick, but it wasn't used in public," says Dr. Adams.

Something else happened to dick. Until the late 1950's, obscenity laws made it illegal to print most curse words -- and that would include dick as penis. Those laws were overturned in a series of different lawsuits -- with the 1959 court case involving *Lady Chatterley's* Lover being the most important.

For the first time, all sorts of "forbidden" words could be legally printed and circulated.

The baby boomers were coming of age during this time, and began to embrace a new linguistic landscape, one full of obscenities. In 1968, at the height of the boomers' counter-cultural revolution, an underground magazine called *The Realist* published the text of a panel conversation about obscenity. Panel moderator and critic Bob Fulford said that using obscenities had become "almost a symbol to a certain kind of young person" and noted how they "use these words all the time and in casual talk."

My Name Is Dick

No one on the panel disagreed.

And as it so happened, this panel was held just a few years before one man, lost in a scandal of his own making, became the first in American history to resign from the office of president. Enter Richard Nixon, whose use of the nickname "Dick" both demonstrates the name's history, and whose reputation, I believe, provided the final nail in Dick-the-name's coffin.

From the very beginning of this research into the name Dick, I wondered what role Richard "Tricky Dick" Nixon played.

A clicking sound-maker from Nixon's failed 1960 Presidential bid.

I had wondered -- was Nixon to blame for its final downfall -- or vice versa -- was the name's downfall the reason Nixon quit

My Name Is Dick

using it?

Like so much with the name and word dick, the truth is -- both.

"Richard Nixon has a part to play," says Dr. Adams, "but with dick, as is often the case with slang, different things come together. You have a number of things happening at the same time."

As it turns out, Nixon's use and abandonment of his nickname Dick tracks with the historical timeline of the name's rise and fall. But there is also evidence that he played a role in disgracing not just himself, but everyone who shared the name Dick. This was the part he played, and it played out something like this.

Nixon was born in 1913, when Richard was the 13th most popular name in the US for boys, and Dick was rising in popularity, heading toward its height as a name.

Throughout his life, Nixon used both Richard and the nickname Dick. Generally, he used Richard with more formal circumstances -- as in his 1937 FBI application, or his early congressional and senatorial campaigns.

Dick he used in less formal circumstances. A college professor and a classmate called him Dick, as reported in a 1958 Saturday Evening Post article, and a 1944 letter to his beloved Pat was signed even more simply, with just "D."

My Name Is Dick

In this way, Nixon used his name and nickname as did many Richards of his generation. But this is where the resemblance ends.

Nixon's first negative influence on Dick the name began with "Tricky Dick." The nickname didn't begin with the 1970's and Watergate. It was the 1950 California Senator's race, and Nixon was running against Helen Gahagan Douglas. Douglas thought Nixon's campaign tactics were underhanded.

As the New York Times says in a 1994 article, "it was in this campaign that Mr. Nixon was first called 'Tricky Dick,' an epithet bestowed by *The Independent Review* in an editorial and picked up by Mrs. Douglas in her campaign."

Dick, already losing popularity, was going to be in for a long free-fall with Nixon.

Unlike any other Dick before or since, Nixon's name was on 5 presidential tickets. Dick was alternately used and avoided and used again, all for political purposes -- by the campaigns themselves, the press, and the voters.

As Ike Eisenhower's 1952 running mate, Dick began as a tagline to what's arguably the most famous slogan in campaign history: "I Like Ike."

After Eisenhower named him his V-P candidate, many buttons started reading "I Like Ike and Dick."

There was some question if Nixon would again be

My Name Is Dick

Eisenhower's running mate in 1956 and so "Stick With Dick" became political buttons at that year's Republican convention. Again, Eisenhower won, and again, Tricky Dick was by his side.

As Roger A. Fischer wrote in his book *Tippecanoe and Trinkets Too*, Nixon had a notoriously low-likeability factor, and by 1960 when he was running for the presidency itself, "(a)nother humanizing tactic was the great prominence given Nixon's nickname, 'Dick,' on campaign items, although some uniquely tasteless varieties of buttons that read 'They Can't Lick Our Dick' -- at least one of them given out by the campaign itself -- probably did little to project Nixon as a latter-day Lincoln."

Though he lost in 1960, Nixon's nickname was not to blame. But those changes in obscenity laws -- coupled with the rise of the counterculture and their love for swearing, would change the name Dick forever, as well as Nixon's future campaigns.

"Unlike 1960, when references to Nixon as 'Dick' were so common, only one 1968 button did so," writes Fischer. Free press and free love had made the meaning of dick as penis pervasive.

Having held a spot since 1900, in 1968, Dick dropped out of the Social Security Administration's top 1000 baby names list. It hasn't returned since.

So in 1960, Nixon embraced his nickname. In 1968, he avoided it. By 1972, the opposition had co-opted it.

McGovern was Nixon's 1972 opponent, and as Fischer

My Name Is Dick

writes, "(n)o national McGovern items satirized Nixon, but buttons created for local groups and for vendors bore such insults as....the monumentally tasteless 'Lick Dick in '72.'"

Dr. Nuessel says that Nixon "was a major inflection point" for the name Dick. And somewhere, hidden away in Dr. Nuessel's attic or garage is one of those anti-Nixon Dick buttons. His reads "They Can't Lick Our Dick." Says Dr. Nuessel: "People who were 'wise' got it. Those who weren't, didn't. It was definitely ambiguous."

The "wise" were largely the young members of the counterculture, the ones recently freed by changes in anti-obscenity laws (as well as their own attitudes) to curse at will.

The rest of America would soon catch up to dick's newly-popularized use as penis.

While extensive research has shown a whole raft of uses, past and present, for dick, I've yet to discover how the name or the word also became synonymous with jerk. I suspect, however, that "Tricky Dick" had something to do with this as well.

After a disgraced Nixon resigned from the presidency in 1974, he still used Dick with those he considered personal friends. But if by then the rest of the country called him dick, it was for different reasons altogether.

"Yes," says Dr. Nuessel, "Nixon gave the name Dick a really bad name."

My Name Is Dick

Nixon never really came clean.

But I suppose I should. See, I have my own personal history with using the word. And not only as my name.

Once I've put away my driver's license and people understand my name really is Dick, the next thing I get is sympathy for my childhood. Especially if the person I'm talking to was born after 1980.

"Oh man," someone will say, "it must have been ROUGH growing up with a name like Dick. You've gotta be scarred from all that teasing."

"Not really," I will say, and it's the truth. My biggest problem was that people thought it was short for Richard, which in my case, it wasn't. I was just Dick, like the boy in our *Dick and Jane* readers at school. Dick was years away from being an issue, bland enough to keep me safe from name-shaming, and common enough to be solid -- I think every "Tom, Dick and Harry" felt this way about it.

I did get teased growing up, but it was by my older brother, and it wasn't for my name. Until Dick ascended (or descended, depending on how you look at it) to the position of meaning jerk and penis, it was the poor Peters of the world who had a rough go of it. In fact, Peter was my big brother's favorite way of teasing me.

I can still hear him taunting me in that sing-songy way,

My Name Is Dick

calling me "Peterhead, Peterhead," over and over. And over and over again. And again.

I remember thinking it could have been worse. That my name could've actually been something as awful as Peter.

Too, I remember learning a toast from a work associate in 1980, when Peter was still the common (but waning) referral to a penis.

The toast went like this: "Friends may come, and friends may go/And friends may Peter out we know/But we'll be friends through thick and thin/Peter out or Peter in!"

That toast turned out to be the last time I ran across a reference to Peter as penis, but depending on the setting, surrounding and company, I still say it today. So I get how the English-speaking world now sighs with relief that they aren't named Dick. I also get how it sounds and feels much better to call someone a Dick instead of calling them a Peter.

"Think about most cuss words you know and use," writes Maddie Crum in a Huffpost article called, appropriately, *Where the F**k Did Cussing Come From?* "There's 'damn.' There's 'shit.' There's the F-word and the C-word. Many of our expletives are four-letter terms, a trend that's so consistent it bears exploration. In his book, (Benjamin) Bergen charted English-language examples, and found that three- and five-letter words were just as common, but most were a single, consonant-heavy syllable — usually one

My Name Is Dick

with its consonants piled on the end."

My personal favorite curse word -- if not my favorite word, altogether -- is f**k. I use it all the time. I like the way it sounds, how the word forms in my mouth and then leaps off of my tongue with unmistakable clarity. I'm not surprised Dick overtook Peter as a swear word. Unlike Peter, Dick has many of the same qualities as my beloved f-bomb, and because of that, I have a confession to make.

I frequently call people Dick or Dickheads.

Despite the many grievances being named Dick has brought me, I confess that I find myself oddly proud not only of dick's varied history, but also that my name has all the properties of my other favorite curse word. But f**k it. Unlike Tricky Dick, yes, I'm coming clean. I take my own name in vain, and am happy that my name is all-purpose, just like the f-bomb. Dick is not only both a proper and regular noun, but it's also as a verb and adjective. Try hard enough, and it could probably could be an adverb too.

Let's take a moment to pause and admire Dick's versatility, not just in its history, but in the here and now of curse words, where it is only rivaled by its f-ing linguistic twin.

"What a Dick!"

"Dickhead!"

"Dick off!"

"Stop dicking around!"

My Name Is Dick

"Whatta bunch of dicks!"

In your greatest fits of anger or rage (usually behind the wheel), you can even combine our language's two most multi-functional curse words to form what is arguably the *pièce de résistance* in all of swearing: "F**ing Dick!"

It's annoying when people snicker about my name, even more annoying when they don't believe Dick is my name, and most annoying of all when they refuse to call me by my name. That's when I take a long, deep breath and think: "Whatta bunch of f-ing dicks about Dick." And then I smile.

Thank God no one names their kid Cornhole, which is what I grew up learning either happens with a corncob in an outhouse, or something two male dogs might do to each other.

No, wait. That's now the name of the popular family-friendly game played at bars, bar-be-ques, and tailgates and involves tossing a bag full of corn kernels at a board with a hole cut into it.

"Hey Dick," a friend of mine called out to me at a recent summer party, "wanna come play Cornhole with us?"

First I snickered, and then I didn't believe them, calling back across the yard to my friends, "WHAT do you want me to play?" When they explained, I then said, "You're messing with me. What's this game REALLY called?"

Aww, f**k. I guess I really AM a Real Dick. But at least give

My Name Is Dick

me this: once I quit my snickering and disbelieving, I could say and play Cornhole as loud and proud as I say my name.

There is nothing to fear in a word.

I am no professor of linguistics, but as I learned about the many other meanings of the word dick, I realized how much I didn't know before. I guess you could say that I had been guilty of "swallowing the dick." That's an 1870s slang term for using words without knowing their full meaning, but now that we all know the truth about dick, we won't be swallowing it anymore. On to other things.

Cornhole, anyone? I play fair. I'm no Tricky Dick.

If Your Name is Dick, Don't Be One

"We'll call the guy Dick; it's the world's most Freudian name." -- Stephen King

He may be best known for his tales of horror, but in my journey to tell Dick stories and better understand writing, I picked up King's *On Writing: A Memoir of the Craft*. Yes, I learned about writing by reading it. When it also taught me that I have "the world's most Freudian name," I began to think about something else entirely.

I began to wonder about my Dick stories. Are they fun? My friends say they are. Entertaining? I hope so -- and you will help me decide. But is there something more? How did my name affect my personality -- and the personality of anyone named Dick?

My Name Is Dick

I have a lot left to learn, but my best start came from Dr. Cleveland Evans, the professor of onomastics at Nebraska's Bellevue University who I introduced in the last chapter. Before him, I had not heard of onomastics before, either. But as the study of proper names it's a real thing, folks. These academics even have their own international council.

As past president of the American Name Society, Dr. Evans is one of several very helpful onomasticians we've been talking to as we sleuthed out the history of the name Dick.

But as I pondered what it meant to have the "world's most Freudian name," I knew we had to talk to Dr. Evans early on. Besides being an expert onomastician, Dr. Evans is also a professor of psychology.

Turns out, how Dicks respond to having their name will vary widely. "There's going to be differences based upon a personality," says Dr. Evans. "People with high emotionality -- they are more likely to come up with something else to use as their name. Extroverts will tend not to care and embrace it. It's about the temperament of the individuals involved."

As for me, I think I'm a mix. I'm an extrovert, and I've embraced my name. But I do care what others think -- or at least I once did.

"Like anything with human nature," says Dr. Evans, "you have to accept all parts of your personality. This acceptance is what

My Name Is Dick

makes someone mature -- and one of the indicators is our ability to laugh at ourselves."

Well okay then. I'm on the right track. I'm definitely setting out to laugh at myself here. But what if other Dicks can't?

"There's nothing morally wrong with changing your name," says Dr. Evans, "But of course you can also try first developing a more positive attitude."

If you're a young Dick, it's not going to be as easy to be positive. "It must be particularly hard for people under 30 with this name," says Dr. Evans. As our Dick history showed (and most Dicks already know) Dick was once a perfectly acceptable name for kids. Not now. If you've faced teasing, Dr. Evans says to "remember the name is much older than its use as a slang term. Many real and fictional people named that are very admirable..."

Regardless of age, though, there's one bit of advice all Dicks can embrace. "If you're not going to change it," says Dr. Evans, "You need to try to develop PRIDE in it."

That's right, Dr. Evans. "Loud and proud" became my motto over the years. I'm feeling like I'm in a pretty good place here with my name, but I have questioned if it's rude to others for me to use it so unabashedly.

Dr. Evans weighed in. "As a social justice matter, if Dicks want to use their names, they should." A social justice matter. The idea is interesting.

My Name Is Dick

Still -- what would Freud himself say about people named Dick?

Dr. Evans chuckled lightly at this question and then answered it thoughtfully, just as he answered all of my questions. (Turns out onomasticians aren't only name nerds -- they are also a pretty nice bunch of people. And smart.)

"Freud is quite guilty of extremes sometimes. He would probably say either that you would act like a jerk because of your name....or obsessively act the other way."

So I guess being a Dick might make some with the name overcompensate by being syrupy nice all the time. I do have a sense of humor and always try to be kind, but if truth be told, I have been known not only as a Real Dick, but also as a real dick.

Maybe it's what happens when you have the world's most Freudian name. Or maybe it's what happens when you are a human being, period. We all can be both good or bad. It's what you choose to make of it.

Case en pointe -- meet Andy Dick. Tricky Dick has nothing on him.

I've had some friends helping me put my stories together, and one of them wanted to do something special to give the project (which started with a blog -- thedickname.com) a fun send-

My Name Is Dick

off. So she goes to Cameo.com, a site where you can request celebrities to make videos for you at a price they name. She looks for, of course, a Dick, and finds comedian Andy Dick. If you look at his featured Cameo videos, they're fairly decent and at least moderately humorous. So for $90 bucks (now $99 at this printing) she makes a request and sends along several notes for him -- things she's hoping he'll say to me.

My friend had heard of him, but didn't know a documentary had been made about him and his notoriously-bad behavior. It's called *Everybody Has an Andy Dick Story*, and my friend was about to get one of her very own.

The video is made on his cellphone, and shot in a spartan room. I guess it was his bedroom, or at least a room with a bed in it. White sheets, white wall -- the whole dark space has this oddly psychedelic blue cast to it. Maybe it's a blacklight he has on, I don't know. All you see is Andy Dick's scruffy face, his head laying on a pillow, his hair going several bedhead directions.

"Dick...Sherrod," he says.

"That's me!" I think when I first see the video, excited. "How cool! Another real Dick -- a famous one -- is talking to me!"

In the video, Andy next scratches his cheek and turns his head to the side.

"It's Andy Dick."

He clears his throat and begins what appears to be an

My Name Is Dick

attempted reading of the notes my friend sent him.

"Your friends at the-dickname-dot-com," he says, pausing for the first of many times. When he says "the-dickname-dot-com," my joy immediately begins to dissipate. He enunciates his words clearly, but also with a six-year-old's whininess, as if he's saying, "YES mother, I've done my homework." He rolls his eyes, and continues after his pause.

"...want me to say good LUCK..." Here there is no pretend legitimacy at all to his well wishes. He's clearly annoyed. "...to you in finding lots of Dicks...to talk..." now he purses his lips and pauses again "...to you, I guess, or your blog. Do you have a blog? The. Dick. Name. Dot. Com." This time when he says the website name, he sounds confused, as if he's attempting to processing it.

He sits up in bed, and for a second I hoped he was going to really get into it.

"....and future Dicks" he says, again pausing and looking away, this time with an eye roll.

Then he stares back into his phone. His eyes are slits. No, he's not into it. He's gotta be high. Or something.

His voice begins to drop to a whisper, his phrases less coherent. "...not just the Richards. I am hoping that all Dicks..." and now he looks around the room, pressing his tongue into his cheek, looking like all he wants to do is finish a very badly done reading and collect his $90.

My Name Is Dick

Then, for a split second, I have another flash of false hope. He giggles a little when he says "...are willing to talk about life..." and then, of course, all hope is dashed as his slurred voice becomes nearly inaudible. I had to put in earbuds and crank the volume all the way up to hear "...with the world's most freudian name. Oh gah. DICK," he says, and then gives me something I can't miss. His middle finger. "Dick Sherrod," he whispers.

Wow. I'm pretty sure this was not what my friend had in mind.

Mercifully, however, the train wreck is almost over.

While Andy has been talking and flipping me off, he shifted around to where you can see a couple of paintings in the background -- they look like they were done by graffiti artists -- but not good ones. Andy Dick, now done with his painfully-obligatory and totally meaningless reading of good wishes, now points to one of the paintings and says, excitedly, "Oh. This painting is about to go up in flames. I'm literally going to light it on fire. Huh." He brings the camera to his face and his voice takes on a creepily sexy tone. "So tune in to that." And as the video ends, the only thing on fire is my friend's hope for a thoughtful gesture for me.

"Dude," I thought, "I don't think I will ever tune into another thing about you again."

But I did, wondering if, like "Tricky Dick" Nixon, Andy Dick

My Name Is Dick

had made the Freudian choice of very badly becoming his name.

I remembered Andy Dick as the comedian who played the goofy and sweet Matthew on the '90s sitcom *News Radio*. I knew he'd had some troubles with the law and addictions, but I'd never registered it much -- it seems pretty commonplace for stars. I had no idea how or to what scale Andy Dick had blown a once-promising career.

After I was sent the video, I Googled him.

One quick search was all it took to show me that, even amongst the most legendary of screw-ups in Hollywood, his failures are of epic proportions.

His is a story of repeated sexual harassment, arrests, addictions, continual rehabs, and blown second chances par excellance.

Amongst his encyclopedic list of failures is a long-since-canceled radio show on Howard Stern's XM channel. I'm a long-time Stern fan (and that alone tells you I'm not an easily-offended prude) so I looked it up. What I found was a segment on Stern's show, one where they played a bit from another show -- a podcast Andy had appeared on after his XM broadcast was cancelled. Andy went on a hate-filled, slurred, anti-semitic rant against Stern, who had done nothing but given Andy another shot at success. All Andy did was blame Stern's Jewishness for his own failings.

I'm not Jewish, but I was so offended that, for as much as

My Name Is Dick

Stern railed on Andy, it was not enough railing to suit me.

I thought about it for a moment, considering how perhaps I could've become my name, too. I found plenty more of Andy's stupidity as I continued my search, but was stopped cold when I found a video of an Andy Dick appearance on Dr. Drew's CNN show, shortly after Whitney Houston's death. It was during one of Andy's many attempts to get clean. Andy was sober. And sobering.

It was a man without the mask of drugs. I could not help, but for a moment, to empathize with him.

I thought of myself, of how I loved me some cocaine in the '80s. How I once loved cigarettes even more. How they almost both wrecked me -- until I gave them up. Both. For good. Years ago.

Me on drugs wasn't me. Except for being a dick. Andy Dick on drugs isn't Andy. Except for being a dick.

Me off of drugs began to accept all sorts of truths about myself. Andy off drugs seemed to be doing the same.

Getting sober was actually the same time I finally decided to embrace my name. It's when I could start saying to people, "No, no, my name isn't Richard. My name is Dick."

For me, I got clean, had built some professional and personal life successes, and by early mid-life, accepted that I am a Dick. According to an PRX audio essay by Nathan Callahan, Andy Dick "embraced his name with such enthusiasm that by high school

My Name Is Dick

he called himself Superdick."

Andy. Andy. You were years ahead of me on the self-acceptance curve there. So no matter how many times you've failed, you're still alive. You can still choose to get and stay clean.

See, Andy, just because Dick is your name doesn't mean you have to be one. Your whole life doesn't have to be one long Freudian slip.

It's a choice, just like Dr. Evans said.

See Dick Work

In my worklife, I attended countless conferences. You know those, large, pre-registration type of conferences where your company has spent good money for you to attend, you fill out your credentials, submit them, and you're good to go. Well -- most registrants are.

As for me, I waited for the phone call.

"Are you Mr. Sherrod?"

"Yes," I would reply, waiting for it.

"I am (just fill in the blank) from the National (just fill in the blank) calling about your registration."

"Yes?" Here it comes.

"I am calling to verify whether you want your name badge to read Richard -- or Dick?" There was always a moment of hesitancy before the caller said "or Dick."

My Name Is Dick

"What does it say on my credentials?"

"It was filled out as Dick, but we thought you might want your formal name on your badge."

Through the years, I've had various reactions to this scenario. When it first happened in the 1990's, I was surprised if not a little confused. But as the years rolled by and the word dick became more and more associated with words penis and then jerk, the numbers and occasions of people wanting to call me Richard skyrocketed.

This is the case for many Richards. Few go by the nickname Dick anymore. Instead, it's Rich, Ricky, Richie, or just plain Richard.

Except for me, Dick is not a nickname. It IS my name.

There was a time when I'd get The Call and want to jump through the phone yelling -- "Are you an idiot? Do you think I am not capable of filling out official documents and credentials correctly? Do you think I am that stupid? Do you need to see my birth certificate?"

But I am a professional, and after I was done silently grinding my teeth and internally cussing and throwing fingers to the person on the phone, I would choose to be polite and start what became The Routine.

"Dick is my real name. That is why it was filled out correctly. I am not a Richard."

Silence on the other end. In that silence, there was always

My Name Is Dick

palpable and awkward shock. Or maybe it was just the caller covering his or her mouth to keep from laughing.

"Okay," finally comes the answer from the other end. "We just wanted to verify. Thank you." Somehow I never had to rush these callers to get off the phone -- they were the ones in a hurry to end our conversation.

For a Real Dick trying to build a career, mundane tasks turned into (often humorous) adventures into patience, ones that revealed things to me about others, and about myself.

In the beginning, as a struggling young man looking for a business break from people I didn't know, I always thought that my hard work and credentials would open up the doors and give me lots of options and opportunities. Credentials and hard work do open some doors, but I have lived long enough now to know that it is success that opens far more. That is why networking and socializing is so important. You just need to find that one person, a mentor, to give you a chance to prove yourself. At that point, your successes will begin to speak for themselves, but until then, getting to know people gives you your best shot to shine. Afterwards, it's still good policy.

Luckily I found that one person within the first 10 years of finishing college. One bit of advice he gave me was to go back to

My Name Is Dick

school for my Masters of Business Administration (MBA). He was right. From that graduation forward, my career took off.

Earning an MBA opened me to global travel, global moves, leadership skills, speaking opportunities and more. You name it. All from just that one person who took a chance on me. My first mentor allowed me to flourish, hone my skill sets, build a reputation in the financial and banking markets, and position me for my biggest successes.

My name was not anything unusual yet.

This may have been changing before my eyes for some time, but I hadn't noticed. My circle of friends and influences from the mid-eighties to 2001 were somewhat limited. I was so enamored and interested in being a part of the growing global economy that my laser focus was on being a part of major companies and taking my finance career to a new frontier. I even left the well-known energy company where I was the chief commercial paper trader to take a position in the tech finance world that would allow me to move to Singapore in the late nineties.

In Singapore, my name was definitely not an issue. And even as I moved into two different companies in finance positions upon my return, it still wasn't.

I was making a name for myself. I didn't yet realize how my name already might be helping to make -- or break -- me.

My Name Is Dick

My second mentor was a global leader and managed business teams in the US, Europe, Asia and Latin America, and she was the very best boss I ever had. She introduced me to what she called "the lunch test." She liked creating fun names for ideas. The simple but powerful idea behind "the lunch test" was that sharing a meal with a potential colleague was the best way to get to know a person and how they might work best, or not, with you.

It was also this mentor who helped me realize the growing notability of my name, and how I could use it instead of running from it.

She created the "Dick File."

This was just as my name was beginning to really take on other popular meanings, and I have never been totally sure if the "Dick File" was intended as a double entendre or not, though I tend to think it was. Anytime I needed to do something, be constructively criticized, or even earn praise, my boss would say "I am putting it in the Dick File," with a clear emphasis on "Dick." Putting it in the Dick File could mean an array of things: that she needed to follow up with me later on something for which I was responsible, or remember something for future reviews, or simply document an activity or incident. Regardless, in many meetings with my trip associates, when it was heard that something was going into in the Dick File, stifled (and not-so-stifled) laughter would follow.

My Name Is Dick

It was the first time I realized my name could create not only embarrassment, but also bonding. I decided to go with it, and I was glad that I did. Soon, I was privileged to be asked to join a global bank I had always dreamed of working at -- and when there, share the secrets of my successes. When I did, my name was part of the story.

When I moved to yet another global bank, I was lucky to find my third and final mentor -- the one who took me to where I am today. She allowed me to really flourish in my skill set and "give back" not only to clients, but also to my chosen industry. I was happy to be a backbone and workhorse for my employer, and at the same time, they gave me the platform to become a master of ceremonies and key speaker at multiple industry events. It was here I felt totally empowered to use my name in opening many speeches and talks to relax the crowd and break the ice. It worked. My career was continuing its upward trajectory and I was having fun, and I did it by embracing my name and its many meanings.

Instead of running from my vulnerability, opening up to my name helped me succeed.

Not that there weren't many times it was a total pain, too.

There is one thing you can expect when you enter into a finance career focused around the treasury: you are going to have your signature and/or facsimile put on bank accounts.

Every banking and financial institution is required to

My Name Is Dick

perform certain KYC (Know Your Customer) requirements on each and every bank account that is opened. Even under the best of circumstances, these requirements are more onerous than a medieval bloodletting. Of course, one of the things that is required is the name of each signature or authorizer of opening and use of an account. I feel you can begin to see a picture emerge here.

When opening accounts, the use of my name went through a regular litany of multiple back-and-forth calls, emails, all filled with incredulous questions. "Is his name really Dick?" or "Is that how he wants his name on the official records? What? REALLY?"

I had one associate who came to dread these calls, and for a long time, thought I was just stubbornly sticking to the use of a nickname, one whose meaning had become more and more socially inappropriate. After much conversation, (and showing her my license, etc.) she did, however, finally come to believe that my real name was Dick. Over the years it was she who gamely fielded most of the questions, innuendos, comments and backlash that each account opening brought. Out of this, we developed a lifelong friendship and still laugh over all the times my name was used -- in both "good" or "bad" ways -- during our time together.

One interesting note for this issue surrounding account openings and my name: I cannot recall one foreign account opening where my name ever caused pushback or additional inquiry. Just as living in Singapore had immunized me for awhile

My Name Is Dick

from the changing meaning of my name, opening foreign accounts again proved that Dick is pretty much an American problem. I am convinced that this has some bearing on my love, to this day, for traveling abroad.

I was always aggressive about searching for my next career move throughout my professional life. And with every move I have made from 1974 until today, I have been lucky enough to say they have all been upwardly mobile. So, when I ran across a recruitment advertisement from another top tier bank in a trade journal basically doing the same thing I was doing but with a "team" twist, more money, and better opportunity, I decided to interview.

The only problem was that by this point in my career, I knew that being a Real Dick was a thing. Sure, I could embrace it with co-workers and in front of friendly crowds. But this was different. I was applying for what appeared to be my dream job, the one that I hoped would be the pinnacle of my career in industry and finance. I would be able to retire after this job and move to someplace sunny and warm, someplace near the water.

So in this case, I squirmed a little when I looked at my name on my resume. But I sent it anyway. I couldn't turn back on who I was now.

It seemed to work. My resume made the first cut, and I

My Name Is Dick

made it through two phone interviews. I was flown in for a face-to-face interview. It was at a nice restaurant, during dinner. The lunch test my first mentor had told me about -- well, it had gone prime time.

I remember walking into the steak house and meeting with the top brass for happy hour first, before the rest of the team showed up. It went well with the leads and I was ready to meet my team peers. The four guys arrived en masse and introduced themselves.

"Hi, Dick Sherrod, good to meet you," I said to each as I shook their hands.

Two of the four responded: "Richard, good to finally meet you in person."

I smiled and said nothing. We were immediately seated at our dinner table and everyone was busy ordering their drink of choice, so I decided to wait to let them know that I am not a Richard.

These people were new to me, to my name, and most of all, I wanted to be their new hire. I wasn't sure when or if I would correct them.

There was the usual small talk about office culture, business plans, and sports scores. I was doing well. So well that after a couple of vodka sodas -- and maybe a glass of wine -- I decided to go for it.

My Name Is Dick

Just before I dove in, I remembered my first mentor saying that an interview isn't just for them -- it's also for you. I needed to know these people could handle the real me, name and all.

So I swallowed hard and announced to the entire table that I needed to set the record straight for them.

Everyone got quiet, and I smiled a little before saying: "I am not a Richard, I am a Real Dick."

They couldn't believe it, as I have come to expect.

"No really, it's true," I said, and of course proceeded to show them my driver's license and current business card.

A few days later, they offered me the job. I took it.

You can make a good impression, I suppose, no matter how much of a Dick you are. Or perhaps you can make a good impression because of it. When you're willing to own your vulnerability, it shows others your humanity -- and your internal strength.

And, well, yes, every now and again, a correctly-timed vodka soda doesn't hurt you in the courage department.

As it turns out, the position was a great fit for me -- I was able to meet that professional goal of helping to formulate and drive a new team to success. My colleagues would often begin a client meeting they were leading (or that I was brought in on, I

My Name Is Dick

swear just so they could do this) by announcing my name for me, and by making sure everyone in the room knew immediately that I was, indeed, a Real Dick.

But soon enough, however, being a Real Dick was going to cause a whole new issue on the job, one I did not see coming, one that no mentor or experience could have prepared me for.

So there I was, late into my career, happily accepting the challenge of a job move which required me to use all my knowledge acquired over the years to be successful. I also accepted that I was a little older than most of my colleagues, and was aware of their regular snickers, laughter and awkwardness surrounding my name. Suddenly I was in front of other peer executives, colleagues and associates where dick was used frequently (like the f-bomb) in the course of conversations. Whenever I was introduced to new people -- whether internally within the business or at a speaking engagement, certain individuals would always come up to me and address me as Richard.

By this point, I was tired of people not listening or assuming I was a Richard. I started using my name as an ice-breaking introduction for myself to every person or audience I addressed. Dick became my trademark and, from at least a professional

My Name Is Dick

perspective, the conversation surrounding my telling the story of being a real Dick was always worth the while.

My position often involved hosting bankers, financial industry peers and colleagues at my office. They would call on me to sell products, financial strategies, softwares, to benchmark practices, do surveys and many other things. I was often asked how someone could find me once they reached my access-controlled floor after becoming validated and checked in at the receptionist. The answer was always easy. "Once you gain access to my floor, head to the north side of the building. If you can't find my office, simply ask anyone for Dick. I am the only Real Dick on the floor." I can't tell you how often that created a chuckle or grin, but it always worked. Everyone knew who Dick was and although there were certainly some other dicks on the floor, I was the only one with the name.

I was comfortable talking about Dick, I was comfortable telling my story, and most of all, I became proud of being a Real Dick.....on many levels.

Of course, this is when I discovered a whole new level of problem with my name -- and it was one that once again, I had not seen coming.

My Name Is Dick

It was early in my new team role, but we had established a unique niche in the bank (and in the industry) as we were not traditional bankers. We had all come from the corporate side of the fence and offered clients advising and consulting from the "corporate" perspective. We also didn't "sell" products and services. We simply advised and worked as a free service to help clients achieve the successes we had all enjoyed when we had "walked in their shoes," so to speak.

We had just been approached by a top-tier bank salesman who wanted to introduce us to a key global client based in the New York/New Jersey area. After September 11, 2001, company security protocols began to require tedious check-in procedures. Typically, the first thing required was for me to surrender my identification (driver's license or passport) and a business card to one of the security officers. An officer would move forward with taking the picture that was to appear on my temporary entry badge, and another one entered my information into their computer system. I assumed that when entering my information, they were not only registering my name, but also performing some type of search for any heinous or criminal activities on my record.

We arrived at the company's headquarters, and everything was going routinely. The team was standing around the security desk awaiting our temporary badges with their newly-minted pictures when one of the security officers says, "Mr. Sherrod? We

My Name Is Dick

have a problem."

I had no clue what that could mean. I had never been arrested. Not even close. My mind immediately began to wander: what if my old drug dealer from 20 years ago or some old friend had mentioned me in some official report that somehow appeared in some FBI-type file? It didn't cross my mind that my name itself could be a security issue. The rest of the team proceeded to take a seat and wait for our escort to lead us to our finance area meeting room.

As I approached the guard who'd said we had a problem, he looked up at me and said, "Our computer won't take your name."

"Huh?" I said.

The guard repeated himself. "Our computer won't take your name."

I was startled and dumbfounded. "What? What do you mean?"

The guard lowered his voice. "Dick," he said, looking around. "I cannot give you badge credentials. The computer refuses to accept your first name."

My only alternative was to drop my name and be "badged" as my middle name, Wendell.

I seethed, but I was also with my colleagues, a bank client, and at the security desk of Fortune 500 company -- one we were

My Name Is Dick

all hoping to work with. Once more I couldn't be a professional and simultaneously cause a scene, although I wanted to.

I laughed instead.

My colleagues couldn't believe it either, but they laughed too and we proceeded to wait for our escort to our meeting.

At the meeting, I told my story to the client. Everyone in the room was incredulous, and as it turned out, my story had once again broken the ice and led to a very successful first meeting. Ultimately I know we made a real difference for both the bank's sales guy and the client. That's usually the best part of the work I liked so much. Not this time.

This time, the best part was that I had a badge reading "Wendell," proof of something I had not known existed before. Folks, name discrimination is real, and this was only the first of several times it would cause me trouble at company security desks.

Perhaps I should have filed name-discrimination lawsuits against these hugely successful companies who banned my name. Had I done so, I may have never had to think about my own finances again.

But then, I would probably have had to sign non-disclosure agreements. And then I would not have been able to tell the story to you. So -- I will take my deal.

Besides, that name badge is one of my favorite souvenirs.

Everyday Dick

Being a real Dick becomes more complicated than I ever imagined.

We were nearing retirement and my partner and I had decided we did not want to end up in Houston, where we were at the time. We knew it needed to be a warm place and near some form of water. We started looking at some of our favorite places: Southern California, New Mexico, the Lake Travis and LBJ areas of Texas. After a trip to Costa Rica, we decided to search for property there. I never dreamed that my name would be a problem.

We have all been through these processes before seeking information on any array of topics. Very routine. I was looking online for properties in Costa Rica, and after finding several listings of interest on a site, I decided to give them my contact information to see what they could find for us. Once my data entry was

My Name Is Dick

complete, I proceeded to click on the submit button -- and that is where it began.

Once I clicked submit, the following response immediately popped up on my screen: "Please don't put bad words into our system." I stared at the screen, a little confused. I reread the entire form, thinking I must have mistyped a "bad" word by mistake. I couldn't find any, so I clicked submit again, and once more got the same response: "Please don't put bad words into our system."

It was then that I remembered my previous issues at security desks, and I realized what was happening. Of course. It was my name their form was rejecting.

I was shocked -- sure, in face-to-face interactions, I had run into problems with my name, but never with anything online. What, was I going to offend a foreign computer server somewhere?

I called my partner into the room and said: "Oh my God. Look at this."

Now we both were stunned. We laughed, got a little pissed off, and then -- reality set in. "I need to fill out an official form and I can't because my name is considered vulgar," I said. "If we move to Costa Rica I may never be able to use my real name again." I imagined what it could be like if we actually managed to purchase real estate in Costa Rica. What if we pulled that off and were then were unable to sign up for utilities, file taxes, or whatever else because my name was considered vulgar in the entire country?

My Name Is Dick

So we started looking in South Florida, where all the real estate agents took my name, where the weather is warm and the water is near, and I could use my name without major issue.

Three out of four ain't bad.

I first began to realize Dick was going to be a regular public problem when all restaurant servers wanted to call me Richard.

Like anyone else, if I am calling ahead to make dinner reservations, I use my name. If I don't make a reservation in advance and just give my name at the hostess desk upon arrival, I still use my name. And whether it's over the phone or in person, I've discovered a secret, one universally true about restaurant hosts and hostesses. They all seem to have hearing problems.

"Dinner for six," I will say.

"Name?"

"Dick."

"I'm sorry -- I couldn't hear you. Can you repeat your name?"

"Dick."

Silence. Then: "Can you spell that, please?"

"D-I-C-K," I say, spelling it slowly.

"Richard?" they will ask. (So evidently spelling is a problem, too.)

My Name Is Dick

"No. Dick."

Pause again. "Um -- what is your last name?" I will be asked.

"Just call for Dick," I answer.

"What?" says the host or hostess. Again the hearing issue. So I repeat myself once more.

"Just call for Dick. I will be the only real one in the room."

Granted, most hosts and hostesses are younger, so it's probably not their hearing. More likely they've just never met anyone who is actually a Dick, much less a Dick that's being a bit of a dick about it.

Giving my name for a table is really just where the restaurant fun begins. While we're in the bar waiting, we play a guessing game. How will we be reached when our table is ready? Will they call my name out like they do for everyone else -- or will they leave the host stand, come find me in person, and tell me? Whoever bets that my name is going to be called out loud is almost always the one who loses. Surprise.

At least we get some personalized attention out of the deal. I am always curious to find out from the host or hostess why. As we follow them to our table, I will ask: "Why didn't you call my name out over the PA system? How did you remember who I was? Was it my name?"

"Yes," they will admit, a little embarrassed.

My Name Is Dick

Don't worry. I'm a good tipper.

It was also here in Florida that I learned that I didn't need to move to Costa Rica to find problems with my name and utility companies. Florida already had those problems waiting for me. I discovered them one Saturday morning when the yard waste truck missed the pickup at my house.

Living in the semi-tropical zone of South Florida means that we continually have to attend to palm fronds and the year-round trimming of foliage. The debris goes out in front of my home to be collected by a special truck on Saturday mornings and then hauled off to I don't know where -- I imagine there must be a giant palm frond mulch factory somewhere. Regardless, it is magically gone each week.

One Saturday in July this process failed. My debris pile was placed on the curb in front of my house, as usual, for pickup. For some reason (I never learned why) my house was skipped. Everyone else's debris pile was cleared. Since I live in a gated, landscaped-controlled community, this of course created an immediate problem with the homeowners association. I got a call accusing me of not having my yard debris on the curb on time (it was) and I had to turn around and call the trash company to complain -- and to get them to make a special trip to clear the

My Name Is Dick

offending fronds before the homeowners association had a collective aneurysm.

Enter life as a Real Dick.

I logged into the trash company's website with my account credentials and they had a place to put in requests, commentary, or whatever to their customer service. I proceeded to input my story of being missed, how the HOA was mad, and to request a pick-up.

At the end of the descriptive message, I had to enter my name, address, phone number and the best way to be contacted if I was needed. Once that information is entered, I clicked on submit to send. It is a fairly simple process, but my submission was rejected. I tried and tried to submit my complaint and request, but it was rejected with every attempt.

With my temper mounting and spouting curse words (as you know I'm prone to do) like smoke from a chimney, I recalled my Costa Rica issues. I decided to try my partner's name instead of mine. It worked flawlessly.

I turned into a fuming maniac and began to look for a contact number for customer service. I wanted them to know that not only had they skipped me and pissed off my entire neighborhood, but I was also unable to submit my complaint and request because of my name, and now I was more pissed at them than my HOA was at me.

My Name Is Dick

When I called and complained, I found yet another hearing-impaired person. After repeating myself multiple times, they finally believed me and took the complaint.

As I watched out my window while my yard waste was carried away, I finally realized that things might have reached a tipping point with my name. That from now on out, I might have trouble living anywhere in the world as a Real Dick. That my name might create problems not just every now and then -- but every day of my life, for the rest of my life, wherever I went.

As it turns out, that's exactly what's happened.

Take a trip to Starbucks, for example. One particular breakfast order turned out to be its own two-for-one ordeal, showing what happens when a Real Dick splices together online and face-to-face interaction. It gets tricky. (Please don't say Tricky Dicky.)

I was on my way to start a full day. In a rush and in serious need of caffeine and a quick breakfast, I ordered my Starbucks from my phone, trusting it would be ready when I arrived.

I should say kudos to Starbucks for not kicking out my online order based solely on my name. Yes that has happened.

And when I arrived at the coffee shop, my order was ready.

So was my barista's apology.

My Name Is Dick

I went to the counter and told her what I was there to pick up. I dig what they can do with some egg whites.

She looked stricken, and glanced at her colleagues who seemed not to notice her obvious distress.

"Sir," she began, almost whispering, "I'm so sorry."

"What," I replied. "My order not ready?"

"No," she said, picking up a bag in one hand and staring at the receipt in her other. "This must be your order. But someone -- something went wrong. Your name isn't on it. Something else is. I apologize."

"Let me see," I said, guessing what the problem might be. "I'm sure it's fine."

She hesitated. I reassured her. She slowly handed it over.

I laughed when I read it. She looked a little relieved, but still apologized again.

"No apology needed," I said. "Nothing's wrong here."

"What?" she said.

"Dick is my name," I said.

"What?" she repeated a little more slowly this time, her relief turning into confusion.

I could tell she was young enough not to remember when Dick was as plain a name as Jane.

"Dick is my name," I repeated.

"Oh - I am so sorry," she began. "I mean, I'm not sorry that

My Name Is Dick

um, that is your name." I grinned a little at her, trying to ease her awkwardness. It didn't help. "I mean I'm sorry that I was sorry that that was your name." She rubbed her forehead.

"Don't be sorry. And don't be sorry you were sorry. I'm used to it."

"Well, okay..." she sounded unsure. Maybe even a little nervous. I guessed she was concerned I would complain to her boss.

I held up a hand. "No worries," I said, taking my order and weaving through the interested-but-trying-to-look-not-interested line behind me.

"I just didn't know that was a real name," I heard her say to the fellow who was next. He'd evidently gotten some entertainment from the whole encounter at the counter.

Smart businesses like Starbucks know it's good to call customers by their names, and bad to use profanity at them. So when a name IS profane, typical customer service rules can go out the window, and in their place, somebody is going to be embarrassed. It took me years not to be the embarrassed one. Now, even if the awkward moment occurs at the doctor's office, I've learned to be, and remain, a loud and proud Real Dick.

The doctor's office incident began with my knees, and when

My Name Is Dick

they started to balk at my regular walks, I knew it was time to visit an orthopedist. The first time I went, I got my forms from the front desk and sat in the full waiting room to fill them out and to await my turn.

As in most doctor's offices, the nurse would stick her head out of the door and call for patients when it was their turn. In the waiting room, all eyes were on the nurse whenever she opened the door.

"Bob?"

"Karen?"

"David?"

"Mark?"

"Maggie?"

And then, finally, me.

"Mr. Sherrod?"

I stood, and everyone looked at me. I think they assumed I was either someone important -- or that I had a terrible first name. I smiled as I walked across the waiting room, and the nurse looked like she was a little rushed to get me away from the crowd.

"I'm Susan," she said, simultaneously sticking out her hand and backing into the hallway, letting the door close behind me. "I will be your nurse today."

"I'm Dick," I said just as the door clicked shut. "Pleased to meet you."

My Name Is Dick

"You too," said Nurse Susan, "Follow me."

We were quiet as we walked down the hall. I followed her into the exam room. I sat as she took my blood pressure and temperature and we chatted some about the weather.

"Well, Mr. Sherrod," she said, looking over my charts. "You're here for knee trouble?"

"Yes, Susan," I said -- maybe with a little more emphasis on Susan than I meant to. I paused. "You know, if you call me Mr. Sherrod, I'm going to think you are looking for my father."

Nurse Susan gulped a little, but smiled and made a slight nod. She said neither Mr. Sherrod or Dick for the remainder of my visit. I didn't push it. The way my knee was bothering me, I knew I would be back.

My next visit, I was prepared. I even got there a couple minutes early, in plenty of time to hear other names called.

"Betty?"

"Randall?"

"Carl?"

"Mr. Sherrod?"

I hesitated and didn't look up from my magazine.

"Mr. Sherrod," said Susan. I could feel her eyes on me.

"Oh, I'm sorry," I said, standing and giving her a little wink, "I thought someone was calling my Dad."

The hall door clicked behind us again. "Will they not let you

My Name Is Dick

call out my name in the waiting room -- like is your boss giving you a hard time about it?" I asked.

"No, no, Mr. Sherrod. I--I just have never known anyone named your name. Normally it's just short for Richard, and I can use that."

"Not me," I said.

"No -- not you. I double-checked before I first called you."

"You know, it's not so bad. I've never known of anyone who used my name to die of embarrassment. In fact, I have been told it's kind of liberating to call my name out without getting in trouble. You can try it."

"Oh gosh," said Susan.

"Ah, c'mon, give it a shot," I said.

She didn't reply, but sat me down in the exam room, and took my blood pressure and temperature. She opened my chart, and shook her head a little. I thought I heard a chuckle before she cleared her throat.

"Well, Dick, how are you today?"

"Susan," I replied, giving her a thumb's up, "Better now." I thought about high-fiving her bravery, but I didn't want to be too over the top. I still think it would have been appropriate, though.

The next time I went to the office was a few months later, and felt in luck that Susan was once again calling the patients back.

"Harold?"

My Name Is Dick

"Larry?"

"Dick?"

I hopped out of my chair so quickly my knee popped loudly. It hurt but I ignored the pain.

"Susan," I said, "how good to see you!"

I've become a regular now at the orthopedic doctor, and Susan has become my favorite nurse of all time. She's great at what she does and we laugh a lot -- often about my name and my latest adventure with it.

Now it might just be my imagination, but I swear, she now calls my name out louder than anyone else's.

"Dick!! You ready?"

I am ready indeed.

Sure, my name now creates hassle every time I am required to fill out a document, register or sign in somewhere, apply for credit, title a home, property or car, or sign up for insurance. Yes, I invariably get some type of call, instant message popup, bad language warning, or refusal of service because I am a Dick. I have had to make so many corrections, affirmations and fulfill so many requests for proof of my name that it is now part of my daily routine. I almost don't even notice it.

But it's too late in the game for me to be anyone other than

My Name Is Dick

who I am, and while I may have to worry about being able to get a doctor's appointment or a dinner table, at least I know I will always have a story to tell at the end of the day.

So I'm going to do what I've done my whole life. What Richard Nixon's campaign buttons long ago once asked voters to do. Stick with Dick.

Even if that means I have to live up to my name from time to time.

See Dick Travel

You can have a getaway from daily pressures, but you can never get away from yourself.

I recently returned from the trip of a lifetime -- or at least mine. India, for a month, served up delights and wonders of all tastes, sights, and types. And along the way, my name turned out to be one of them.

When getting through airport security went off, for once, without a "Sir, is this really your name? Please step to the side," I thought for a fleeting moment that this might not only be the vacation of my dreams, but also, a short respite from being a Dick.

In some ways, it was. Many of the Indian locals I encountered didn't know enough English, or at least enough English slang, to bat an eye when I introduced myself. That was refreshing.

My Name Is Dick

But to get on a tour bus filled with mostly English-speaking folk was like being right back at home.

"Hello," said to the fellow next to me as I took my seat, "I'm Donald, but folks call me Don." He extended his hand.

I shook his back. "Nice to meet you. I'm Dick."

"Now there's a nickname," said Don.

"It's not a nickname...my name is Dick," I said.

"No," he replied, incredulous.

And so I pulled out my license for the first of many times on that bus. It became such a thing that I briefly considered asking the tour bus host to make an announcement. The host, while Indian, knew enough English to enjoy the humor of my name -- without the embarrassment that us Americans surround it with.

"I bet that it is fun to have a name like Dick," he said, his accent thick. He grinned.

"It can be," I said, and stopped. India, beautiful as it is, still offers many sights of poverty. I wasn't about to complain about something like my name.

The bus was filled with all sorts of tourists, and was like a small, rolling slice of our deeply divided America. The political factions were clear and boisterous. Never mind that this trip had nothing to do with politics.

It was here I discovered how Dick can bring people together like little else.

My Name Is Dick

Our tour bus stopped at St. Thomas Cathedral in Mumbai. Built in 1718, it stands as one of the oldest (and most awe-inspiring) buildings that the British erected. We all quietly milled about the sanctuary, with its soaring, arched ceilings and stained glass.

That's when Don (whose politics and background I had quickly learned are about as different from mine as is possible) came jogging up to me. Don was very excited and a little breathless. "You gotta see this," he said, and took me by the arm.

Dick, as Memorialized in St. Thomas Cathedral, Mumbai, India

We crossed the cathedral. "Look, look," said Don, pointing up to a memorial plaque for one George Dick, evidently a very successful chap from Britain who had come to India as part of the

My Name Is Dick

storied East India Company and died here in the early 1800's. "Another Dick in church," he said, sounding almost like an excited schoolgirl.

I looked at him, and was thinking about being annoyed when he said, "Well, this is just the best thing. You couldn't miss it." Don, a man who may have been forced from his recliner to take this trip, a man with which I had little else in common, had found a moment of genuine joy. Because I'm a Dick.

I smiled. Who am I to deny someone a moment of happiness?

"It would be something if you were related," he said.

"Dick is my first name," I said, pointing again to the memorial. "It's George's last. Maybe he's related to Andy Dick?"

"Yea, yea, I know. But still," said Don, patting my shoulder. "Who is Andy Dick?" he added.

"Just a guy with the name," I said, smiling.

If you're a real Dick, you cannot escape it. Not even when you travel back home again. But you can embrace it.

For me, "back home" is Tennessee. And a trip there spells more Dick adventure.

For the uninitiated, "being a Vol" means I graduated from the University of Tennessee, home of the Volunteers. Technically,

My Name Is Dick

anyone from Tennessee could call themselves a Vol -- since we are known as The Volunteer State, our residents having enthusiastically volunteered for various military calls starting with the War of 1812. But really, only those Tennesseans who went to UT claim the title of Vol with a Big Orange fever, one unsurpassed by any sports fandom in this country.

(An aside, and with all apologies to the University of Texas, WE are the Real UT. Formed in 1794, the University of Tennessee was here almost a hundred years before the University of Texas. Heck, we were the University of Tennessee before either Tennessee or Texas were even states.)

In the fall, "Big Orange" Saturdays are a sacred ritual in Knoxville as well as across the state. Neyland Stadium is a South Eastern Conference shrine and is consistently rated one of the largest in the nation, and during home games is always packed, even if the team is not having a good season. Trying to get tickets to the beautiful stadium on the Tennessee river is difficult, for cheering for the Vols is a religion for many Tennesseans.

Football Saturdays when I was an undergrad at the Real UT were an event not to miss (and still aren't). The partying would always start on Friday nights and continue, especially if the Vols won, well into Sunday morning. I knew this from the time I was a boy -- for I not only went to UT, but Knoxville, where the university is located, is also my hometown. Growing up in Big Orange

My Name Is Dick

Country, and being a Knoxville native, at UT student and frat boy, nothing topped the home football experience every Saturday throughout the fall.

I graduated from the Real UT in 1972, and took my first job out of town. My career kept me away from Big Orange Saturdays for almost 40 years. And yes, my immediate family all considered me a bit of a black sheep for it -- in this way, I am the only wayward sibling in my immediate family.

A few years ago, I finally saw I could come home for a Big Orange Saturday, and I asked my brother if he could get tickets for the game. I planned my trip to be in town for a game in October and made a reservation to stay at a former World's fair site hotel. My brother came through and got tickets for all of us (me, my brother, my sister and all significant others) to see the Vols take on the Georgia Bulldogs.

Not wanting to miss a minute of the weekend's fun, my partner and I flew into Knoxville on Thursday before Saturday's game. We got a rental car (no problems with my name) and proceeded toward the hotel -- we needed to get checked in, cleaned up, and ready for drinks and dinner. Since it was a ballgame weekend, the hotel was completely booked and very busy, so for us there was no question we were going to valet the car when we arrived at the hotel.

That is where the fun began.

My Name Is Dick

When we opened the door and began to unload our bags, the valet service asked me for the reservation name and a name for the car in order to bring the car around whenever we asked for it. I told them my last name, as that's what is normally required, but they also wanted my first name. With cars lining up behind us, and with people all around the crowded hotel entrance, I sighed and prepared to get a few head turns. I sat my bag down.

"My first name is Dick," I said. I saw a couple of heads turn.

"What?" said the attendant.

Oh, perfect, I thought. This was not the welcome home I had hoped for. "DICK, D - I - C- K," I spelled out. I am so accustomed to this routine that I have become pretty numb to it, but then I realized there were lots of people within earshot who weren't. I glanced around, wondering if I knew any of them. The valet was looking down, covering the grin behind his mouth, and other guests were giggling as they rolled their suitcases by me and into the hotel. I was grateful that I didn't know a single one of them.

But then I decided I wasn't going to get upset. Not this time. So I chose to take the situation as the humorous moment those around me saw it as. "And, yes," I added, using my rather-loud Go Vols volume level, "I am a real Dick. I am NOT a Richard."

A man gave me a thumbs up as he went into the hotel. If I hadn't been tied up at the moment, I would've chased him down

My Name Is Dick

to see if he was a real Dick too. We are few.

Instead, I turned back to the valet, who was clearly embarrassed for both himself and for me, and yet also smiling ear-to-ear.

"For real?" he asked.

"I'm as real a Dick as there is," I replied. I don't think he would've been any more surprised than if I said my name was Penis. Course to him, I suppose that is exactly what I was saying.

As luck would have it, the valet attendant that initially serviced us at check in was on duty much of the entire weekend I was home. Every time I saw him, he would smile, snicker and barely look at me. But I always got my car -- and I always asked for it by my first and last name.

Funny thing is, that weekend, for as proud as I was to be a Vol, finally once more cheering in the stands in a sea of Big Orange in that beautiful stadium, I looked at my family. I felt a bigger-than-orange pride for being the only Real Dick in the bunch.

India, Asia, Europe, South America, Tennessee. Everywhere I've traveled or lived, I have enjoyed graciousness, good food, and laughter. But 15 years later, there is one place which combined them all in a way which stands out above any other. Somehow it seems fitting that, thousands of miles from my home country, it

My Name Is Dick

had to do with my name.

Our story takes place at a remote restaurant tucked away in a forest. Since this is England, it was pouring rain. Since it was a work dinner after a long day, it was dark, too. So yes, folks, it was indeed a dark and stormy night in the forest. Childhood stories tell you that you can make all sorts of discoveries in this setting. Fairies. Witches. Wizards. Robin Hood. Me? I found Spotted Dick.

I should tell you that even before my colleagues and I arrived at this woodland restaurant, we had all been working hard to maintain professional composure. Americans traveling to the British town of Leeds (or points east of it) will discover that while the locals claim to be speaking English, their accents are so overwhelming that one is inclined to think they are lying. From the time we touched down at the airport until we left the next day, our entire, tired team was giggly over our difficulty understanding our native tongue as it was spoken there.

The people I traveled with was a team of business-suit executives, and usually we were a buttoned-up bunch. But the combination of jet-lag and miscommunication kept us all having to turn our heads and cover our mouths. No way did we want the very-poised Brits we had just met and were working with see us laugh whenever one of them spoke.

If you've ever gotten tickled during a funeral or in a theater during a tear-jerker, you understand. We knew it was highly

My Name Is Dick

inappropriate to laugh, and none of us wanted to, but once it started, it was a highly-contagious bug, one no one was immune to. Not even our boss. In fact, the harder we fought the laughter off, the more it sought to overtake us. Somehow, though, we succeeded. Our new business associates invited us to a dinner.

We arrive at the restaurant in the woods with our new business associates, and we are wet, hungry, exhausted and giggly. Professionals that we are, we still kept our behavior in check, even under the influence of a cocktail or two. Even though it meant we had to stare at the floor to do so, we managed not to create a scene through all of the main dinner courses.

Then we made the mistake of deciding to order dessert.

This was 2004, well into my becoming comfortable with jokes about my name, often making them myself. The American coworkers I was traveling with, the ones who had spent the entire day struggling not to laugh, were the same ones who were part of all the Dick jokes back home.

We asked for a dessert menu. We each were handed one.

As we were reading the offerings, there were instantaneous, simultaneous, glances between my American peers and me and then, what we had suppressed all day could no longer be held at bay. Without any of us saying a word, we all broke out into fits of uncontrollable laughter. It was unstoppable.

Our hosts looked at us, and then each other, stone-faced

My Name Is Dick

and confused as we snorted and gasped and tried, in vain, to regain our lost composure, much less place our dessert order. I don't know who was more embarrassed -- us or our hosts. We could not even catch our breath enough to apologize or explain what was so funny. Our waiter stood there for a moment, silent.

What prompted this behavior? The grand dessert menu had an item of which none of us ignorant Americans had ever heard. Spotted Dick.

Not only had we not heard of it, one of my colleagues made the further mistake of asking our poor waiter what it was. With each question, answer, and glance, our laughter got more and more uncontrollable and in the company of local people and the new business associates we had just met. One of us had to be excused for the restroom.

And so it was that here, on a dark and stormy night in the forest, me and a few of my fellow Americans discovered a completely different level of giddiness and laughter. It was a Dick-incident they have not let me forget. For weeks after, it was hard for any of us to look at each other without breaking into laughter, and to this day none of us have fully recovered. We still talk about it whenever we get together.

Preparing to write this story, I have been searching, searching, searching, for the restaurant where it all went down. It was a place called The Beech Tree. Yes, there are restaurants with

My Name Is Dick

that name in Great Britain, but not one of them seemed to fit the rural, wooded place I remember. I reached out to restaurants of that name, and they agreed they weren't the place I was looking for.

And then I found it, on a lone TripAdvisor post about a restaurant called The Beech Tree, located in just the right spot. It made me sad. The restaurant is closed.

See, once me and my co-workers finished making a complete nuisance of ourselves, explaining our behavior, we expected to lose the professional respect of our new associates. We also expected everyone within earshot to be offended, including and perhaps especially the wait staff. Instead, we got offered a keepsake menu. Signed by most of the people who had borne witness to our foolishness.

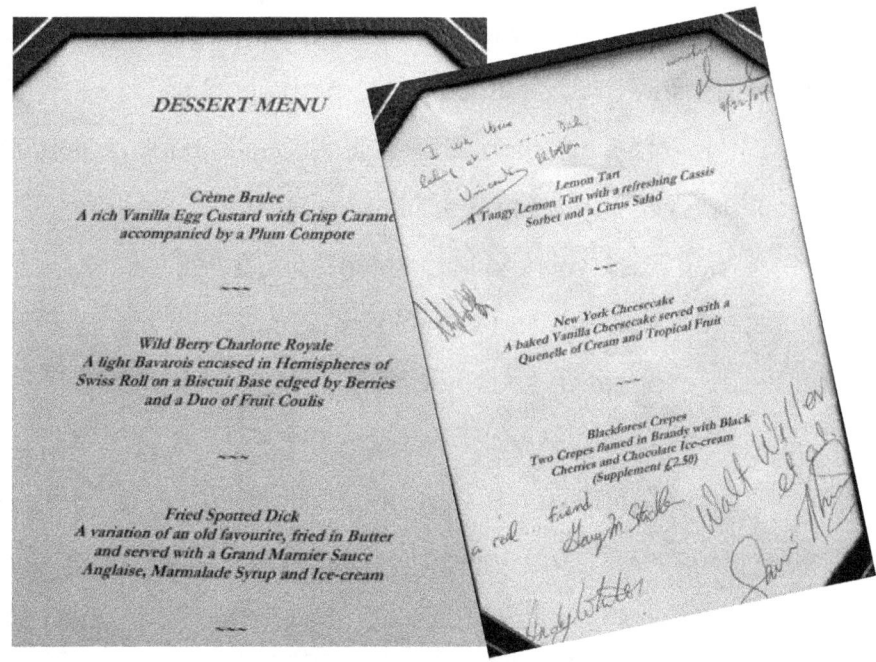

My Name Is Dick

Everywhere I've traveled, I have enjoyed graciousness, good food, and laughter, yes. But no spot on earth ever offered it in more abundance than this one. And I have the menu to prove it.

As we continue our travels with Dick, I'd like to give you a souvenir: a little tale about, well, souvenirs. Whenever I travel, I always hit the kitschy little gift shops where they have gifts with names on them. My favorite was the fake license plates, and once upon a time, I could find them. My goal was to get all 50 states. But that's not going to happen, I've come to accept.

So over the years, it's become a bit of a mission to find something, ANYTHING, with my name on it. I might even go for a fake plastic cow paddy if it had "Dick" printed on it.

I go into a gift shop, and if I look long enough, eventually a salesperson will walk up to me. Oh man. Their lucky day.

"Can I help you find something?" I'm asked.

I might pause, and sometimes consider not saying a word. But desperation drives you to do things.

"I'm looking for Dick," I reply.

If the salesperson is someone older than 40, I will get a grin and a response of something like: "Sorry, sir, we don't have your

My Name Is Dick

name."

"In your storage room, perhaps?" I usually ask, holding out a bit of hope.

If the salesperson is under forty, I get pretty nervous when I say I'm looking for Dick. I worry that one day, some salesperson will whip out a cell phone and call the cops, saying there's some creeper in their store asking for inappropriate things. Still, I keep trying. Despite the risks and disappointments, I don't give up hope easily.

Sometimes it's the kindness of people who make the difference.

Kelly is my step-son's wife, and is aware of the challenges surrounding my name. She has taken up the cause and has begun looking for Dick, as well. I have been touched by this kindness, but never more than when this came in the mail recently:

Of course, I was thrilled. Props first to Kelly for searching for this Dick gift, finding it, and sending it to me. And then, you gotta throw some love to the Natural Bridge Caverns in San Antonio, Texas, too. Apparently, they, like Kelly, aren't afraid of Dick!

I had almost given up all hope for Dickname items until Kelly came along and found this. I was inspired. If there's one name-shame-free zone, (or at least a place that hasn't changed their gift item stock since the 1990's dare I hope there is another?

My Name Is Dick

Now, I returned to my search with renewed vigor.

And as I write, I am on a trip to New Mexico. I sit here, a smile on my face, a tear in my eye, and a Dick on the table.

So now -- evidently not one but TWO small gift shops in Texas and New Mexico are less afraid of Dick than the world's largest soda-maker.

Clearly, the west is still wild.

The TSA, however, is decidedly not.

I will end my travel tales where many of them begin. At the TSA counter.

I know from personal experience, the TSA doesn't do Dick. They won't even SAY Dick.

People hate the TSA. And for good reason. Under the guise

My Name Is Dick

of protecting us (the efficacy of which is debatable), the TSA and its airport security measures cause incredible slow-downs in getting to your plane, bizarre travel item restrictions, and worst of all -- they make everyone in the security lines feel like criminals. Getting through a security checkpoint feels more like getting you're processed to go to prison instead of on a plane for a trip somewhere special.

Perhaps I should not be surprised that being a Real Dick further complicates my relationship with the TSA. But I was surprised, for I discovered this in a small midwestern airport, long before I knew my name was going to be a daily issue or even a professional challenge. Years before it became impossible for waitresses to call out my name for my table, the TSA had a big old problem with my name.

I learned this when I was working on a local government consulting gig with an associate in Tulsa, Oklahoma. We had enjoyed a great week and were headed toward the airport for our trip home. At the time, it was still commonplace to print your boarding pass at your hotel rather than having it on a phone app. (For some it may still be).

Having arrived at the airport a couple of hours prior to our flight home, my colleague and I had made it through the security gauntlet relatively unscathed and had decided to grab a bite to eat before boarding. As we were sitting at the restaurant we heard

My Name Is Dick

(what was to me) a strange announcement over the airport speakers: "Richard Sherrod. Please return to the TSA security area for a lost item."

I looked at my colleague and said: "Well, that's weird. Someone is in this small airport with my unusual last name, plus their first name is Richard. He may not be a real Dick, but still. What are the odds?" We chuckled a little and continued to sip our cocktails. Our conversation had moved on when the announcement came on again: "Richard Sherrod. Please return to the TSA security area for a lost item."

My colleague and I looked at each other and discussed it some more. I decided that it was just too much of a coincidence in such a small airport that there would be another Sherrod, much less one that had a first name of Richard. I decided to play it safe and took myself up to the TSA counter.

"You have been paging a Richard Sherrod," I said. "My name is Dick Sherrod and I just wanted to be sure you really are asking for Richard rather than Dick."

The TSA officer didn't respond, and instead took me by my elbow and escorted me over to the TSA's private office. "Sir," said the officer, turning to me, "will you repeat yourself to my supervisor?"

So I did. "I heard your announcement for a Richard Sherrod. I'm not a Richard -- I'm Dick Sherrod -- but I want to

My Name Is Dick

make sure you aren't calling for me."

The TSA supervisor and officer stared at one another, and then at me. Expressionless, and without uttering a single word, the supervisor handed me my printed boarding pass. I must have dropped earlier it in the security checkpoint. I suppose getting a full-body search throws me off a bit.

You would think that these people -- who for a living, scan the contents of every carry-on, put you through detectors which investigate what's underneath your clothes, and then put their hands all over every person, young or old, who sets off said detector -- you would think that these people, of all people, would be able to say the name that's printed on the ticket they are trying to get to its owner, instead of announcing the name they WISH was on it.

Yeah. I was getting a little annoyed by their silent treatment. So I asked the supervisor why they had not paged for Dick Sherrod. Again, the supervisor didn't open his mouth. I repeated my question one more time, and one more time, got zero response. Well, the supervisor blinked.

"Aren't you going to say anything?" I asked. Even to that question -- silence.

At this point I knew exactly what was happening. I pulled out my driver's license and passport. "These," I said, "MUST MATCH the name on my boarding pass. My name is D-I-C-K! Why wouldn't

My Name Is Dick

you call my name out?"

It was at this moment I was shown the door.

I stood outside the office, grateful I had my boarding pass, and at the same time, more than a little pissed off by their rudeness and the general embarrassment of it all.

More than anything, I was simply amazed that these officers would not say a word to me -- forget explaining why they wouldn't announce my name as printed on the boarding pass. I mean, I'm required to use my legal name when I travel. These are the guys that enforce those laws. And yet they can refuse to say the name I'm required by them to use? What?

Maybe I should have reported this incident all the way up the chain, but after returning to the restaurant, telling the story to my colleague, and paying our bill, it was time to board.

"Boarding pass," said the airline attendant at the gate.

I handed her the now-rather-crumpled boarding pass. As she compared my name on the pass to my driver's license, I saw a flicker of a smile cross her face.

Once again, I couldn't help but laugh.

No matter where you go or what situation you are in, it is the one thing which can make your travels, and life, easier.

You Can't Have a Dick and a Smile, But You Might Get a Lyft

The soda giant is famously inclusive -- as long as it's profitable.

All I want is a Coke with my name on it.

And, truth be told, I'm not yet ready to laugh about it.

When Coca-Cola began its "Share-a-Coke" campaign several years ago, even the marketing industry was amazed. People scoured every shop they went into, looking for a bottle with their name on it, or the name of someone they knew. I was one of them.

I found the names of friends, but given my souvenir-shopping problems, perhaps I should have known better than to hope for my own.

As a die-hard, long-time Coke fan, however, I think of Coca-Cola as not only the maker of my favorite soda, but also as

My Name Is Dick

the company that wanted "to buy the world a Coke." The 1971 commercial is widely regarded as having the greatest song in advertising history. If anyone had enough love in their hearts for me, it was Coca-Cola.

Convenience store by convenience store, my hopes dwindled. No, it appeared, you could not #shareacoke with Dick.

I get it. My once perfectly-acceptable name has been hijacked to mean penis, or, at best, jerk. Even I use it that way. It's understandable that Coca-Cola wouldn't have "Dick" bottles sitting on shelves -- any more than they would have "Sh*t" or "F*ck" bottles out on display.

Still. I was disappointed. I love me some Coke, but I chalked it up to another of many Dick-related issues and forgot about it. That is, until a few years later, when I learned you could go online and order a customized bottle.

I jumped on it, and excitedly put in my request. I was immediately told my name was "offensive."

I replied by email:

```
To: shareacoke.support@coca-cola.com
Sent:07/22/17 16:48:50
Subject:Thank you for contacting Share a
Coke
First Name: Dick
Last Name: Sherrod
Nature of Inquiry: Other
Comments: I am appalled at your note that my
REAL name is considered "offensive." I am
```

My Name Is Dick

not a Richard! My given name is Dick. I want a Coke bottle with my name on it! Help!

    And Coca-Cola responded:

From: Shareacoke Support <shareacoke.support@coca-cola.com
Subject: Share a Coke Customer Service
Date: Sun, Jul 23, 2017 at 11:14 AM
Hi Dick,
Thank you for contacting Share a Coke Customer Service.
I'm so sorry to hear that your name was rejected. There are many restrictions for names for trademark and legal purposes. We are sorry that your name was not accepted.
If you have any additional questions, please feel free to contact us again.

    Once again, I let it go. It's just a bottle with my name on it, right?

    But more than ever now, I began paying attention to Coke's advertising campaigns, how the company touts its inclusive ways. In 2018, their Super Bowl ad "A Coke For Everyone" received praise for celebrating LGBT Americans. For 2019's Super Bowl, Coke was again lauded for its ad which "Champions Diversity and Inclusion." In the months after, Coke profiled its Chief Diversity and Inclusion Officer, announced they were raising a "Rainbow Flag at Atlanta HQ in Support of the LGBTQI Community," and risked a boycott in Hungary for ads featuring same-sex couples.

    I should have been thrilled with Coca-Cola's inclusion and

My Name Is Dick

diversity initiatives. Instead, I felt burned and marginalized, and never more so than in the summer of 2019 as Coca-Cola kicked off its "unlabeled" campaign for Diet Coke.

The campaign asks us to "imagine a world where we aren't limited by the way others label us." I've spent years using my imagination and sense of humor to keep from being limited by the ultimate label, one I had no say in receiving. My name.

Coca-Cola, purveyor of "unlabeling," has slapped me personally with a label: "offensive." Twice. Just this week, they rejected my second request to buy a Coke with my name on it, citing its "offensive" nature.

So no, Coca-Cola isn't about "removing labels." It's about courting the buying power of a movement to improve its bottom line. As we look to spend our dollars on companies we believe in, buyers would be wise not to mistake smart marketing for authentic beliefs. It's often hard to tell the difference. Unless the company is Coca-Cola, and you, like me, happen to be a Dick.

I'm not going to give up. Instead, I'm going to ask the world to help me buy a Coke. THAT's the real thing. You can find the petition by going to Change.org.

What perfect timing for my preferred ride share provider, Lyft, to make a major faux pas. Just as I am getting this book ready

My Name Is Dick

for publication, I get an email that my real name, Dick, does not meet their "community guidelines" and asking me to update my name so they can be "respectful" and create a "comfortable" ride for all.

As it turns out, a kerfufle ensued. All sorts of names were banned by Lyft's algorythm, and they took to social media. Of course, the story then hit mainstream media. I did go in to re-verify my name as Dick and then, as did most of the "banned" names, I got an apology letter from Lyft. They realized they screwed up. At least they did apologize. Much better than Coca-Cola.

Concluding Thoughts

I suppose some of you might be wondering why I took the time and effort to produce this book. It was an opportunity for a little self-introspection and documentation of a real Dick life well lived. I have run across so many people (especially since 2001 and the age of of millennials, gen Xers, Ys and Zs began) that are so surprised by my name that I have been asked repeatedly for my stories. This has been especially true since I began to tell everyone that I was going to write about these dick issues and incidents. Ironically, it is the very people from which I have had a story develop that are always the most interested in reading them. It is the hodgepodge of daily incidents that happen seemingly spontaneously that has driven me to fruition. I trust I have created something from which you can get five minutes of joy and perhaps a lesson of life.

My Name Is Dick

I leave you with some more lyrics from my fellow Tennessee native, Dolly.

I hope life treats you kind
And I hope that you have all
That you ever dreamed of
And I wish you joy and happiness
But above all this, I wish you love.

Because you must learn to love yourself first, before you can love anyone else. Self-acceptance is paramount.

Having a name like Dick brings baggage, but as Dolly might say: "It is my coat of many colors."

My name and dick stories will endure and continue. Each day brings new gifts and rewards.

But...a final reminder...PLEASE DON'T CALL ME RICHARD! As journalist Linda Ellerbee once said:

And so it goes.....

About The Author

Dick Sherrod is a former business executive whose life and "Dick" tales all began in the hills of East Tennessee and have subsequently been sown around the globe.

After years of prodding from friends and colleagues, TheDickname.com and blog was where his storytelling journey began, and he remains on a quest to find other Dicks to join him.

He's a super-friendly guy. Just please, don't call him Richard.

My Name Is Dick

www.ingramcontent.com/pod-product-compliance
Lightning Source LLC
Chambersburg PA
CBHW060205050426
42446CB00013B/2998